STONE LANTERN ESSAYS:
services for the collapse of the living room carpet

by

Marlene Kamei

Plumbers Ink Press
Taos, New Mexico

FIRST EDITION: March 1980.

Book designed by nonope press & designs

Graphics by Janet Cannon

Library of Congress
Catalog Card No.: 79-91969

Kamei, Marlene
    Stone Lantern Essays.

Taos, N.M.: Plumbers Ink Press
75 p.
7911   791031

ISBN 0-935684-02-6

This book is dedicated to all my former Creative
Writing and Communications students at Leeward.

INTRODUCTION

The "exercises" offered here were first developed in my Communications classes at Leeward Community College in Hawaii. My own involvement with Zen Buddhism had led me to a dissatisfaction with traditional teaching methods. I had come to the conclusion that the most important thing any "teacher" can do for a "student" is to try to find a way to provide experiences by means of which the student can contact the source of his own creativity.

Thus I devised these visualizations and exercises; I like to call them experiences because they must be experienced in order to be understood. One can talk about or conceptualize creativity endlessly without much result. In fact, my experience has been that conceptualization is worthwhile only insofar as it eventually leads one to realize its limitations; it is at that point we can begin.

We are all artists naturally; the will to create is inherent in our nature and will manifest itself if allowed to. We may not all be composers or painters or poets, but we are all artists in the sense that we are creators of our own lives.

Most of us, however, failing to realize this, end up with our lives mangled and bungled in various ways, wondering if life has any meaning at all. And, if so, how come we missed finding out what it is. Our creativity becomes blocked off, ignored simply because we do not know how to find it and maintain contact with it. In fact, most of us don't even know it's there or have forgotten about it. And we end up frustrated, angry, neurotic people merely *reacting* to whatever happens "to" us.

As artists or creators of life, we do not need to go any further than ourselves to find the material for our creation. It is always there. The body and everything around us is the material, and our "creative genius" is the agent through which our actions, behavior, the forms in our minds, life itself, are manifested.

The person who is able to touch this source of all possibility is able to cut through the forms of conventionality, conformity, programmed ideas about identity, what he or she is capable of becoming or doing, and so on, and become free to manifest his creativity. The person who is able to contact his own "creative genius" becomes free to create himself, to bring forms out of the silence and darkness and manifest them in the world.

Though it is difficult to verbalize, what seems to happen when one touches this source is that he begins to understand the essential emptiness of the self. What we thought we were simply doesn't exist, and it is such a relief to discover we don't exist that this illumination basically frees us. Our so-called "self" is not the elements out of which we are made; rather these elements are the material with which the true self in its essential emptiness creates. The discovery of the true emptiness of the self tends to have the effect of removing the blockage, of providing a feeling of security and fearlessness.

There is a Zen saying that goes, The enlightened man lives as if he were already dead. It is said that simply hearing this is enough to enlighten those who have ears to hear, but to the average person it sounds bizarre or even sinister. It is not either; it is simply a way of saying let go of the ideas about yourself that you have accumulated like a shell around you. The self is not this or that; the self is essentially empty, but a form of energy that is capable of manifesting any possibility.

These "exercises" are suggested as ways (if they are actually done, and not just talked about or thought about) to help break through some of our conventional ideas about who and what we are, and get to that source of all possibility.

They were developed in the late 1960's and early 1970's, and perhaps now ideas of joy/love/ playfulness may seem a little bit naive. But I am sad and distressed at the ideas of doom: ideas that are ugly and essentially against life and joy, that I see manifesting around me. The time has come (again) for those who are on the side of life and joy to work consciously and creatively to manifest a cosmic myth of joy. And so I offer these humble little experiences for whatever good they might do, and if even one person finds them useful or is freed even a little bit by having come into contact with them, it will have been worthwhile to share them.

May all beings be well.
May all beings be happy.

MK

STONE LANTERN ESSAYS

"You live in illusion and in the appearance of things. There is a Reality. You are the Reality. But you don't know it. If you wake up to that Reality, you will know that you are nothing, and, being nothing, you are everything. That's all."

Kalu Rinpoche

Keep a small mirror by your bed. Every morning when you wake up, look in the mirror and say to yourself, "Who is this stranger? I have never seen this person before." Then give yourself a new name for the day. Do not tell anybody the name. Give yourself a new name every day, but never tell anyone your secret name.

Compose, in your mind, songs to celebrate the sunset. Never sing them out loud to anyone.

On the morning after the first snow, go outside for a walk. Take a dry branch with you and wipe out the footprints you leave behind you in the snow.

Ask all your friends for pictures of themselves. Make a collage with the pictures and hang it in your living room. Show it to your friends. Keep the collage a long time. When your friends have new pictures taken, ask them to put the new pictures onto the collage when they come over.

One night when there is a full moon, get a bucket of water. Take it out into your garden and set it in a position so that the moon will be reflected in it. Lean over the bucket and look at the reflection of your face as long as you want; then dump the water out of the bucket and onto the plants in your garden.

On the night of a full moon in September, walk alone through the city streets or a country lane. Pretend you have no name. Pretend the wind has no name. Pretend the trees have no names. Walk as long as you want. Walk all night if you want.

On a windy night in autumn, go out into your garden
and let the wind tangle your hair.

Find a lot of old pictures of yourself. Paste them on heavy cardboard backing you've covered with gold or silver foil. Tie strings of varying lengths to them and attach all the strings to a holder so you will have a mobile. Hang the mobile in the wind and let the strings become tangled. Untangle them if you want.

Design a symbol that stands for you. When writing to your friends, use the symbol instead of your name as a signature. Take as long as you need to choose the symbol; it should be one you know is exactly right.

Find a stone for your garden. Search for the stone as long as you want. Search everywhere until you find the right stone. When you've found it, put it in your garden exactly where it should be. Move it as many times as necessary to find the right place.

Take little bottles with corks to your favorite place in the country. Uncork the bottles, and during the afternoon let the bottles fill up with the spirit of the place. At sunset, cork up the bottles and take them home with you. From time to time, when you feel the urge, uncork one.

One day when you are having a pleasant day on the beach, stay until evening. When the red of the sunset is reflected on the sand, choose several pebbles along the beach. Take them home with you and keep them in a safe place until you have made a bag for them.

Sew a small draw-string pouch of dark blue velvet. Put the stones in it. Carry them with you wherever you go. When you are tired of doing this, take the stones back to the place where you found them. Wait until sunset again, then dump the stones from the bag back onto the beach. Take the velvet bag back home with you. Burn it.

Close your eyes. Picture a summer day. See yourself walking through an endless green field. Imagine a rainbow in the distance; walk slowly toward it, then under it. Then picture another rainbow in the distance. Keep picturing rainbows and walking toward them and through them. Each time you do this, try to walk under at least one more rainbow than you did the last time. Do this as many times as you want. When you are tired of doing it, don't do it any more.

Picture yourself walking down a long dark passage-way. Imagine you can see a light at the end. Keep walking toward the light, but let it recede before you so that you never reach it. Concentrate on this exercise as long as you can. When you can't do it any more, stop.

Look for the strongest tree you can find. Look as long
as you want. If necessary, travel to different places in
order to look for the tree. When you finally find the
tree that satisfies you, pick twelve leaves from it and
string them into a necklace. When you wear the
necklace, imagine you are wearing the strength of the
tree.

Sit in your garden on a summer night. Close your eyes; imagine you are growing roots into the ground. Let yourself grow tightly to the ground, so tightly you cannot move. Imagine the wind blowing against you. Feel how strong you are in the wind. Do this as long as you want.

Close your eyes and imagine yourself chasing a horse. You must catch it. Chase it down a road, over a hill, through a pasture. Concentrate on every detail. See every flower, every blade of grass as vividly as you can. Smell the flowers and the trees. Chase the horse until you are so exhausted you cannot continue.

Find a shady tree. Sit down under the tree; forget about the horse. Lean back against the tree trunk with your eyes closed. Relax. Feel the tree against your back. Let your mind drift.

Suddenly you feel something near you. You open your eyes. The horse you've been chasing is standing docile before you. If you wish, you may ride it all the way back home, slowly, paying attention to everything along the way.

On the day of the spring equinox, go to a stream somewhere in the country. Look for a stone in a place where the stream is flowing very fast. Remove the stone from the water and take it home. Keep it for as long as you want. From time to time when you are alone in the evening, look at the stone, then close your eyes and think of the swiftly flowing stream where you got it.

Every day for a month do one thing you have never
done before.

Look through your closet. Pick out the clothes you
don't wear any more. Cut them into animal patterns.
Sew them and stuff them. Give them to the children
you know.

On your birthday, bake a cake and invite several of
your friends over to share the day with you. Put a
ring in the batter and bake it in the cake. Whoever
gets the ring in a piece of cake should keep it and on
his or her birthday do the same thing: bake a cake
with the ring in it and let the person who gets the ring
keep it until his birthday and so on.

Collect a lot of old magazines, especially ones with good pictures. Cut out the pictures and use them to make collages. Make the collages on pieces of cardboard about 8½"x 11". Whenever you are invited to a friend's house, take one of the collages as a gift for your host or hostess.

Plant parsley seeds in a large pot. Let them sprout. Nurture them until they've grown large enough to transplant into smaller pots. Then give them to your friends. The next time you have your friends to dinner, ask each one to bring some sprigs of parsley for the salad.

On the first day of winter, decorate your house with boughs of evergreens. Hang evergreen boughs over the doors; put them in vases and tie some together and lay them in the corner of your bedroom. Let the smell of evergreens permeate your whole house.

When the evergreens have dried out, burn them in your fireplace if you have one. If not, take them somewhere in the country and burn them in the open air.

Gather more and decorate your house again with fresh evergreens. Do this until the first day of spring if you wish.

Invite several of your friends over for a candle light Christmas Eve party. The whole evening should be spent by candle light. Set attractive arrangements of candles all about the place where you live.

Decorate your Christmas tree with things from the earth, things you have gathered and kept through the other seasons for this celebration.

Prepare a gift for each of the friends you've invited, perhaps a poem, a small collage you've made especially for each person or a small plant you've started from a cutting off one in your garden.

When your guests leave, invite each one to take a lighted candle as a special parting gift.

Invite your friends to celebrate the summer solstice with you. When your friends arrive, give each one something from your garden, a flower perhaps, or a small pebble. Ask your friends to keep these things as remembrances of this day until they are tired of remembering.

Find a small piece of wood you like. Sand it until it is smooth and satiny. Keep it on a table or a shelf in your house. Touch it whenever you want. When you are tired of it, give it to someone you think would like it.

Late in the summer get a variety of different fruits and a bottle of light white wine. Make a large fruit salad, chill the wine and invite several of your friends to lunch.

Pour the wine and before eating ask one of your friends to make a toast to the summer harvest.

Don't use all the fruit for your salad. Keep some in a large wooden bowl. When your guests leave, ask each one to take a piece of fruit.

Invite some friends over for the evening. Serve tea and fortune cookies. Make your own fortune cookies beforehand and put haiku poems that you've written inside them. Then spend the evening writing haiku with your friends. The subject for your haiku might be "things that are empty."

For two days take all the clocks out of your house.
Watches too. Put them somewhere out of sight. Don't
think about them.

Sometime when you are driving across a toll bridge, pay your toll then give the attendant an extra toll. Tell him it is for the person in the car behind you. Do this only when you do not know the person in the car behind you.

Choose at random ten names from the telephone directory in your town. Send each of the ten people the following telegram. Do not sign your name or any other name to the telegram:

congratulations stop is nearly
stop of course stop night plus
tax stop appointment

BANK
OF
AMERICA

On a night when there are going to be a lot of falling stars visible from where you live, invite your friends over for a star-watching party.

When your friends leave, present each one with a flower. It should be a small flower, preferably star-shaped, but use whatever is available in your part of the country.

Close your eyes and imagine you are a black bird flying slowly through the blackest night sky you have ever seen.

Imagine you are enclosed inside an eggshell. Do not panic or struggle. Slowly, carefully break away the shell a piece at a time. Do not burst out suddenly. When you have completely broken away the shell, step gently but firmly on all the pieces. Keep stepping on them until they are completely pulverized. Then see yourself slowly walking away. Open your eyes whenever you are ready.

On the night of a full moon, preferably in autumn, go out into your garden. Look at the dry and withering plants. Feel the cold wind on your skin. Imagine this is the last night of your life. Do whatever you want.

Close your eyes and imagine your body is plastic and able to take any shape. Feel the wind molding you. Do not resist its light pressure; take whatever shape happens.

Imagine yourself falling in space, circling slowly down through the clouds like a petal falling to the ground. Take a long time falling, as long as you can. Then imagine yourself landing on grass; feel the afternoon sun on your skin. Relax as long as you want.

Close your eyes. Imagine floating through space on a huge hand. Relax, secure in the knowledge you will not fall, and float as long as you want.

Imagine yourself alone, floating in a boat on the ocean. Relax. Float on the waves. Enjoy yourself. Keep floating until you arrive somewhere. Let the place where you arrive be a surprise.

Close your eyes and imagine you are swimming underwater. Look at the fish, the plants, the coral. Watch yourself moving through the water effortlessly, gracefully. When you are tired, swim slowly out of the water and onto a warm sand beach where you can relax as long as you want.

Buy a bottle of wine. When you and your friends
have finished drinking it, keep the bottle. Put a candle
in it. Some winter night light the candle. Put your
favorite record on. Listen to the music and watch the
candle burn. If there's a moon, look outside at the
moonlight on the snow. Imagine you are the burning
candle. Relax and feel yourself slowly melting away,
burning into the air. Put the candle out whenever you
want.

One day in April, after the trees have leafed out, pick
a leaf from a tree in your garden. Lay it on the palm
of your right hand. Imagine the blood circulating in
your veins is circulating through the leaf. Picture this
as vividly as you can. When you are tired of doing it,
stop. Keep the leaf until it has withered; then bury it
in your garden.

On a day in winter go out of your house early in the morning. Walk through the lanes and streets in the snow. Let the cold creep up your nostrils and into your ears. Open your mouth so the cold can go in. Make up a secret name for the cold. Give yourself the same secret name.

Some summer day lie down in a field of grass. Feel the warm sun. Close your eyes and imagine your body slowly melting away until it is completely gone. Let it disappear slowly, an atom at a time into the earth. Look around at the flowers with that part of you that is left after your body has completely melted away into the earth.

Make up a secret name for the snow. Then give the
secret name to the wind and make up a new secret
name for the snow.

Imagine you are lying on the ground outside and it is snowing. Let the snow cover you completely, then picture yourself leaping up in slow motion. See yourself shouting and dancing but, as if you were watching a silent film, there is no sound. Everything is white and silent.

Imagine your death vividly. Accept the death you have imagined as real. Every morning when you wake up, before you go about your daily life, remind yourself you have already died.

On a night in summer sit alone in your garden watching the fireflies. Detach yourself from all feelings of heaviness and attachment to the ground. Imagine you are floating among winking stars. Do this only for a while, then close your eyes and listen to all the night sounds around you. Become an empty house through which the sounds of the breeze and the crickets drift.

Close your eyes and imagine riding the wind on the back of a dragon. Let the dragon circle the globe and show you the whole world. When you are tired, land somewhere and stay in that place as long as you want. If it is not the right place, have the dragon take you somewhere else. Keep doing this until you find the right place.